The

Five-
Minute
Fundrai$er

Also by Tom Ralser, CFA

ROI For Nonprofits: The New Key to
Sustainability

Asking Rights: Why Some Nonprofits Get
Funded (and some don't)

Developing Your Asking Rights

The Traditional Fundraisers Coloring Book

Tom Ralser and/or Capital Strategists Group,
LLC trademarked terms:

The Five-Minute Fundraiser™
Asking Rights™
Investable Outcomes™
Invest-Driven Model™
Organizational Value Proposition®

**A Simple Way to Make Fundraising
Easier and More Effective**

The
Five-
Minute
Fundrai$er

Tom Ralser

That Dog Won't Hunt Press ❖ Georgia

This book is done with love and thanks for my son, Willem, who says my eyes look like pickles.

The

Five-
Minute
Fundrai$er

The
Five-
Minute
Fundrai$er

The Journey Begins

Once there was an ambitious young woman named Marley who was looking to make a difference in the world.

She wanted to work with a purpose-driven organization: a nonprofit that was having an impact and changing lives.

She wanted to harness her passion.

She wanted to find meaning in her every day work.

She wanted to apply her particular skill set to an organization in ways that would both support its mission-based activities *and* align with her life's goals.

Her quest to find this type of organization led her to research urban areas, rural areas, and every type of community in between.

She discovered organizations in urban areas that provide job training, help with addictions, and facilitate affordable housing.

She learned more about rural area organizations that provide access to health care, workforce training, and school programs.

She found organizations that help the poor: some distribute medicine, some provide clean water, and some offer education where none existed before.

She met with organizations that help animals, work for a cleaner environment, aid abuse victims, and support the arts.

She spoke with those that help children and those that help the aged, religious organizations and secular organizations.

She visited large organizations with many offices, small organizations with a single location, domestic organizations, and international organizations.

She met with organizations that struggle for funding and those that have more money than they need.

She spoke with staff, board members, and volunteers.

She did her best to get a full view of the entire spectrum of nonprofits. Some seemed to be thriving and expanding. Some seemed to be struggling just to keep their doors open.

It became clear this quest to find a nonprofit that was an ideal fit for her might be more difficult than she had originally envisioned. She realized that while some organizations appeared to be fulfilling their mission (i.e., meeting the needs of those they served), others were spending enormous amounts of time, effort and even money on fundraising...so much so that it took away from their ability to help those they were supposed to be serving.

The more she reflected on what she had learned through her research, the more it became apparent that a built-in conflict seemed to exist for nonprofits.

They had two distinct sets of 'customers' to keep happy.

One set was obvious: those who received the direct benefit of any program or service such as food, medicine, training, etc.

The other group—those who contributed the funding to make possible an organization's programs and services—was more subtle, but no less important.

The organizations that effectively served both were those that seemed to be making the biggest difference in the world.

As Marley thought about all the nonprofits she had encountered, she realized one of the organizations doing a great job of serving both 'customers' was located near to where she lived.

She decided to visit this organization the next day.

Marley went early with the hope of getting an appointment with the Executive Director and was willing to spend all day waiting for just 20 minutes of his time.

After stating her name and the reason for her visit, Marley was told the executive director was in a meeting and would be unavailable for the rest of the day.

The receptionist asked, "Would you like to speak with the Director of Development instead?"

"Sure," Marley said, "if that's the person responsible for raising money for the organization?"

"Yes," he answered. "Janet is the person responsible for making sure we have enough funding to do what we do…to keep our doors open and fulfill our mission."

"I would love to speak with her," Marley replied.

When Marley arrived in Janet's office, she found the development executive at her desk with a red pen in hand, marking up a document.

"What can I help you with?" she asked.

"I've been researching nonprofits around the world," Marley began, "to find one that really makes a difference so I can be part of having an impact and change lives."

"I hear that a lot these days from younger people," said Janet. "And I have yet to hear of a nonprofit that says it doesn't make a difference. Can you be a little more specific?"

"In my search for the right organization," Marley explained, "I have found that they seem to fall into three groups.

"The first group does a great job of fulfilling their mission, but they always seem to be distracted by the need to raise money.

"The second group is very good at acquiring funding, but spends so much time doing so they fall short of fulfilling their missions.

"The third group seems to strike a balance between mission fulfillment and funding procurement, which are complementary, allowing both sets of 'customers,' as I call them, to be happy.

"Your organization seems to fall into this third group," Marley continued, "and I would appreciate the opportunity to learn how you achieve this balance as well as how my skills might be useful in support of the organization's mission."

"You're very observant," Janet remarked with surprise. "Many very educated people with career-long experience working for nonprofits could not have put it more succinctly.

"In fact, one of the greatest management minds in history—Peter Drucker—was the first to describe nonprofits as more difficult to manage since, unlike for-profit companies, they do indeed have two sets of customers: primary and supporting. Drucker warned that neglecting either group could have disastrous consequences."

Marley beamed, "It sounds like I am talking to the right person!"

"Well," Janet offered, "I can certainly talk to you about how we do things in the Development Department, but I think you also need to meet with our Executive Director, John. He has the larger perspective on the secret to our success while I interface with our investors more often."

"Your 'investors'? I thought your organization is a nonprofit?" Marley questioned, looking confused.

"It is," Janet responded. "*Investor* is how we—in this organization—describe what most nonprofits call a *donor*. For us, the term *investor* is much more accurate. But I'm getting a little ahead of myself."

"I love the term *investor*," Marley said. "I was a finance major in college and have a thorough understanding of the overlap of accounting and economics. It sounds like your organization operates where for-profits and nonprofits intersect."

"Well, not really," Janet corrected. "We are very much a nonprofit in our tax-exempt status, structure, mission-based focus, and operational needs, including raising money to keep our doors open. Where this organization is different is in *how* we raise money. That's where we borrow terminology from the for-profit sector."

"Can you tell me more?" Marley prompted.

"Let me see if I can get you on John's calendar," Janet offered. "I know today is not possible. He is meeting with our Executive Committee, which includes some of our most valuable investors because they share with us their time, talent, *and* treasure.

"Let me have your cell phone number and I will let you know by the end of the day if I can get you in to see him tomorrow."

Before Marley got back home, she had a text from Janet: "You can see John tomorrow at 9:00 a.m. Be prepared to spend the entire day here."

The Five-Minute Fundraiser

Marley was very excited.

As she approached the reception area just before 9 a.m., the young man seated behind the desk said, "You're here to meet with John, our Executive Director."

"Yes, I am," said Marley. "I'm really looking forward to learning more about the organization, especially how it raises money differently than other nonprofits."

"Yes, our Five-Minute Fundraiser mentioned to John that you picked up quickly on our use of the term *investor*," he said.

"Your Five-Minute Fundraiser?" echoed Marley.

"Yes, that's what we call Janet," he said.

Just then, John walked up, introduced himself, and ushered Marley into his office.

"Please, be seated," he said. "Janet shared with me that you have a more educated perspective on how some nonprofits perform better than others."

"Yes," said Marley. "I've searched all over the world to find an organization to work for that is making a difference.

"But I have to ask: why is Janet called a Five-Minute Fundraiser? I don't have real-world experience in fundraising, but from my research it seems like the process takes longer...even years?"

"Oh, that's true," John replied, "but Five-Minute Fundraiser refers to certain concepts that—if kept top of mind—position our organization as a vital part of the community and help us raise mission-critical funds in relatively little time."

Marley was quickly realizing that fundraising has a much broader context in the nonprofit world than she thought.

And, as John shared more about how he managed his organization, she noticed he kept coming back to certain concepts over and over, using words like *investors* and *investment* just like Janet did.

He also mentioned something she had never heard of before—*Asking Rights*™—and said they are the key to his organization's success.

Keeping
Five-Minute Fundraiser
concepts top of mind
positions an
organization as a vital
part of the community
and helps raise
mission-critical funds
in relatively little time.

"What, exactly, are *Asking Rights?*" Marley inquired. "I've never heard of them before."

"Good question," said John. "And I'm not surprised, despite your thorough research of the nonprofit sector, that this is the first you've heard of them.

"But they are so much a part of how we raise money for our programs and services that I sometimes forget they aren't common knowledge, or commonly practiced, in our industry.

"Let me tell you a little story that will make this concept crystal clear.

"Years ago, when I first became the Executive Director here, we focused on the 3 Gs: galas, giveaways, and golf tournaments. Those activities seemed like a good idea at the time, but they are transactional at best.

"What I mean by that is, while we raised enough money to keep our doors open, we spent so much time planning for the 3 Gs that we had little time or energy left over to do two very important things—serve our primary customers through mission fulfillment and truly engage with our supporting customers to ensure they continue their involvement and investment.

"In fact, it became almost impossible to determine if we were actually raising more money than it was costing us to raise it, especially once staff time was included.

"When I started to personally visit our largest donors—we called them *donors* back then—to ask for increased funding to really raise the bar on what we were doing, a theme started to appear in their responses. They were all open to giving more money *if* what we delivered was what they wanted to see happen. And, at that point, they were skeptical of our ability to do so. In other words, as an organization, we had not yet *earned* the right to ask them for greater financial support."

"Ah, so that's what *Asking Rights* means," said Marley. "The right to ask for more money."

"Basically, yes, but it's more complicated than that. Developing an organization's *Asking Rights* takes time, and it takes a commitment from the entire organization. More important, though, is the fact that they have to be earned."

"This is certainly something I would like to learn more about," Marley prompted. "Can we talk more about *Asking Rights*?"

"Certainly," John said. "But I would like for Janet to join us. *Asking Rights* are a core element that allow her to be our Five-Minute Fundraiser."

John walked Marley down to the conference room where Janet was waiting for them.

Six sheets of paper hung on one wall. Three of the sheets were blank and hung one each to right of a sheet with writing on it. The first sheet with writing said Credibility, the next one with writing said Fundraising Skills, and the last one with writing said Outcomes.

John began with an overview of what he wanted to accomplish.

"Janet, this young lady has impressed us both and, with the way we are growing, her industry research and skill set may be an asset to our team. With that in mind, I think it's worth our time to explain, in detail, how we do fundraising. We can always use another Five-Minute Fundraiser."

"Agreed," said Janet. "We've been so successful with our programs recently that we are probably leaving money on the table with our investors. Besides, I'm eyeing retirement in the not-too-distant future."

"Don't say that, Janet," John chided good-naturedly. "The demand for what we do is outpacing our capacity, both in square footage and talent. I'm thinking that a capital campaign is in our near-term future."

"I was thinking the same thing," said Janet. "So, let's use our time with Marley to explain the basics of our fundraising process in the context of a capital campaign."

"Perfect," replied John. "Let's get started."

"The reason they call me a Five-Minute Fundraiser," Janet began, "is because I keep the three Ingredients required for *Asking Rights* in mind, knowing each produces a Critical Fundraising Advantage.

"These advantages help us raise more money in less time, bring our investors closer to the organization, and set up a sustainable funding model for future mission-based needs.

"When done correctly, *Asking Rights* also ensure our organization maintains its role as an important community asset.

"But let me take a step back and first define *Asking Rights.*

"They are the ability of a nonprofit to deliver Outcomes that are valuable to investors."

Asking Rights
are the ability
of a nonprofit to
deliver Outcomes
that are valuable
to investors.

Janet noted the look of confusion on Marley's face. "There are a lot of operative words in that single sentence," she said, "so let's go through each one.

"*Deliver* means a nonprofit must actually follow through on its promise to achieve results, not just repeat its mission and goals in glossy marketing materials.

"*Outcomes* means those results need to be expressed in terms of how they impact their primary customers' lives, not just measures of activity that describe how the money was spent.

"*Valuable* means the Outcomes need to be meaningful to those who invested to make them possible.

"And *investors* refers to those who contribute their time, talent, and—most of all—treasure. We use the term *investor* instead of *donor* because *donor* implies charity and charity signals many of the wrong things."

"Wrong things?" Marley echoed.

"Yes," answered Janet. "In our experience, if people see themselves as *donors* and view giving money to a nonprofit as a one-off 'charitable act,' there is little to no relationship to the actual impact of that donation and little to no expectation of the nonprofit except to 'do good things' with the money. It also means an organization might need to take money from anyone—at any time—for anything...assuming it's even remotely mission-related. They feel they can't afford to turn away funding given they don't know when or how—or if—they will interact with that donor again.

"The term *investor* signifies a much more strategic and connected approach to mission-focused funding and, most important, it personifies the expectation of results.

"When we deliver valuable Outcomes, we have earned the right to ask investors for significant funding, hence the term *Asking Rights*.

"And when we deliver Outcomes investors value, we have earned the right to ask them for money again, so it becomes a sustainable funding model."

So far, the idea of *Asking Rights* seemed like common sense to Marley. "Isn't this how every nonprofit raises money?" she asked.

"Unfortunately, not by a long shot, or they would be more successful," said John. "Remember when I mentioned the 3 Gs: galas, giveaways, and golf tournaments?

"The amount of time organizations spend on these things is mind-boggling. And while the staff is busy planning for them, they don't realize that most of the money raised is transactional—in small amounts—versus transformational, and certainly not anything one would consider sustainable."

"I'm not sure I understand," Marley said. "Your model makes sense. It's logical. It's simple. It obviously works for your organization. Why don't more nonprofits use it?"

"That's a great question," said Janet. "I wish we had a good answer. I think it goes back to the old way of raising money, a way that has been promoted by many of the so-called 'experts.'

"I've found that many of these 'experts' never had to really raise money to keep an organization's doors open. Or they had the power of a large institution or big marketing budget behind them. Those scenarios aren't really applicable to the vast majority of nonprofits rolling up their mission-focused sleeves every day."

"What do these 'experts' say you should do?" asked Marley.

"Where do I start?" answered Janet. "It basically boils down to a few basic points.

"First, they rely primarily on emotional appeals. Think of all the late-night commercials featuring starving, crying children or abused pets or disabled veterans. The examples go on and on, but the point is the same. They want to shame or guilt you into giving money.

"Second, they preach that the person asking for money and the person being asked for money must already be acquainted. While that certainly can help, it is not the imperative these 'experts' make it out to be. Their scenario would have you believe the rapport between specific individuals is the reason money is given, and we fundamentally disagree with that.

"We believe, at the end of the day, people give money to nonprofits because of the Outcomes they deliver.

"And that's how an organization should look at things. It's the results that count, not specific connections between only certain people. Executive directors come and go, but—if a mission is needed and supported by the community—the organization lives on."

People give money
to nonprofits
because of the
Outcomes
they deliver.

"Now that I have a better understanding of *Asking Rights*," said Marley, "what are those Ingredients you mentioned?"

"Perfect segue," said Janet. "Let's jump into them.

"There are three Ingredients to *Asking Rights* and they form an easy to remember acronym: CFO.

"You'll see I've written them on these sheets of paper: C stands for Credibility, F stands for Fundraising Skills, and O stands for Outcomes.

"The important thing to remember in all of this is, if you keep these three Ingredients in mind, they greatly simplify the process of raising money for an organization. That's how I became known as the Five-Minute Fundraiser."

"She makes it look easy," John said, nodding toward Janet, "but it took a few years and a decided shift in people's long-held beliefs about fundraising to make everything so concise."

The Three Ingredients

The First Ingredient: Credibility

"**C**redibility," Janet continued, "is the first Ingredient of *Asking Rights* and it's important for several reasons."

She wrote the word Confidence under Credibility on the sheet.

"Credibility gives our funders confidence in so many ways. It assures them we can fulfill our mission…that we know what we're doing. And it makes them feel we are good stewards of their money, which is very important for the next time we ask them to financially support a strategic initiative."

The second term she wrote under Credibility was Board Recruitment.

"Our Credibility is what makes people want to volunteer as members of our leadership team. It ensures our Board is made up of the 'right' people—those who offer their time, talent, *and* treasure, who have strong reputations and significant influence in the community, and who can, especially in a capital campaign, make a lead gift that sets the tone for a successful effort."

The third concept she wrote under Credibility was Team Building.

"Credibility makes it much easier for us to recruit—and retain—quality talent, and investors like to know that our staff is happy and committed to our cause.

"In fact, our Credibility is likely what led you to us," said Janet, looking directly at Marley.

Marley nodded her agreement. "Your organization's reputation in the community definitely drew me to your door."

Janet continued, "So how do we maintain—even grow—our Credibility?

"First and foremost, our track record for mission delivery is key. When people learn of our consistent and long-running impact in the community, our Credibility is reinforced. We didn't just start a nonprofit on the vague notion that we wanted to 'help people.' Ideas like that are easy; executing ideas takes hard work.

"Second, the needs of our primary customers are met. Having been around for 25 years now, our organization has helped thousands of people, and a lot of the people we've helped over the years sing our praises. This not only helps more people who need our services find us, it also helps potential investors find us. Current and potential investors are far more likely to engage with us if they experience our impact with their own eyes and ears.

"Another thing that helps grow our Credibility is low turnover. It signals a positive work culture and supportive management team. It also allows us to build and protect our institutional knowledge base, which in turn makes us more effective in fulfilling our mission.

"In fact, John and I have each been here for 17 years!"

Marley was intrigued with this last statement given she was just starting her professional journey.

"Isn't that an unusually long tenure for senior leaders in an organization like this?" she asked.

"Well," said John, "it might be, but we love what we do. We've also built such a good team. They work well together and are always looking for creative ways to improve our mission delivery and enhance engagement opportunities with current and potential donors. So, there's a lot of incentive to stay."

"While all that is very true," quipped Janet, "I think—now that we've done the really hard work to create a sustainable funding culture—I am seriously eyeing retirement. It's time for me to pass the torch."

John and Janet both turned toward Marley who realized, in that moment, she really wanted to be a Five-Minute Fundraiser.

She sat a little taller in her chair and leaned into the knowledge being shared with her.

Janet stepped to the wall and wrote down another phrase under Credibility.

"The next thing that helps us grow our Credibility is Good Fiscal Management. It is so very important for sustainable fundraising efforts.

"Can you guess why?" she asked Marley.

"Because nobody wants to see their investment in an organization wasted?" Marley offered tentatively.

"Exactly!" cheered Janet. "Although I would say it a bit differently. We ask people for their hard-earned money. They trust us to do good things with it. If we violate that trust, we will—most likely—never be able to ask them for money again.

"That brings us to the next point about growing our Credibility: Successful Fundraising Campaigns. It's amazing how success breeds success. Because campaigns involve so many people, they are an invaluable way to boost Credibility. This boost allows an organization to accomplish things many think are impossible, like raising more money than ever."

Marley asked, "But how many buildings do you need? Isn't that what a capital campaign is for?"

John answered, "Capital campaigns aren't just for buildings today, but that's still a very common misconception.

"In the past, most campaigns were for buildings, and the accounting profession may have inadvertently promoted this idea by calling a building a capital asset, which—as you'll know from your finance studies—is something that is depreciable.

"These days, a capital campaign refers to an effort that employs multi-year pledges toward a significant financial goal, regardless of whether the money will be used for physical structures or for programs and operations."

Marley shook her head. "So many of the things I'm learning today seem to fly in the face of old school perceptions."

"Just wait until we start talking about Fundraising Skills!" agreed Janet. "But let's get to the last important thing that helps us improve our Credibility:

Visibility in the Community. External awareness of our mission and impact helps build our brand, keeps the needs of our primary customers top of mind, and reinforces our position as a community asset, which helps us retain current investors and recruit new ones.

"In fully adopting the concept of *Asking Rights*, we had to embrace the effort of constantly reminding people that we are an important part of the very fabric of the community…an irreplaceable asset.

"Outcomes, the third Ingredient we'll talk about later, help a nonprofit express its mission as an investable community asset."

At this point, Janet had filled up the Credibility page, so she stepped up to the blank sheet right next to it.

"Now for the most important part of each Ingredient," she said.

"Keeping in mind all we've talked about up to this point, the Critical Fundraising Advantage of Credibility—

and how it supports me as a Five-Minute Fundraiser—is that it gets me in the door."

Janet continued, "For example, in a feasibility study, the first and very vital step before launching a capital campaign, it helps me get the initial interviews needed to assess how much financial support is out there for whatever it is we're trying to fund.

"It gets me past the gatekeepers who limit access to the decision-makers. It helps me get to the right person in a corporation to lead our campaign. And it allows me the luxury of convening small groups of community peer leaders to get things done."

"Wow," Marley said. "Who would have thought that one word—Credibility—would help you do so many things! But, in the way you've explained it, it makes complete sense."

"That's the beauty of being a Five-Minute Fundraiser," Janet agreed. "It focuses me on what's important in the eyes of our investors."

Credibility Takeaways

Credibility is important because it:
- Instills Confidence
- Assists in Board Recruitment
- Promotes Team Building
- Highlights Good Fiscal Management
- Sets Up Successful Fundraising Campaigns
- Increases Visibility in the Community

What grows Credibility?
- Proven track record for mission fulfillment
- Attracting and retaining community leaders as board members
- Attracting and retaining quality staff
- Proper stewardship of investments
- Successfully—and consistently—raising money
- Positioning as a critical community asset

What is the Critical Fundraising Advantage of Credibility?

It gets you in the door.

The Three Ingredients

The Second Ingredient: Fundraising Skills

"**F**undraising Skills are the next Ingredient," Janet continued.

"It's easy to think that being a Five-Minute Fundraiser is all about this Ingredient, but it's not. In fact, the third Ingredient we'll discuss today— Outcomes—is probably the most important to get absolutely right in the eyes of the investor. But all three must be in place for an organization to earn *Asking Rights*.

"So, like we did with Credibility, let's start with *why* Fundraising Skills are so important.

"First and foremost, Fundraising Skills allow the other Ingredients— Credibility and Outcomes—to be monetized. By that I mean this Ingredient is what turns the Credibility you worked so hard to develop…and the Outcomes on which the organization spends so much time and energy…into sustainable funding for the organization.

"If you think of the three Ingredients of *Asking Rights*—Credibility, Fundraising Skills, and Outcomes—as a three-legged stool, you can't leave one leg out or the stool will tip over."

Marley thought to herself, "Of course a person has to have a fundraising background—and probably years of experience—to be successful at separating people from their money."

Aloud she asked, "This is where the 'five-minute' part turns into years of experience, right? I mean, how can all of these skills you are about to explain be learned, or even applied, in five minutes?"

Fundraising Skills
allow the other
Ingredients—Credibility
and Outcomes—to
be monetized.

Janet qualified her response, "They do take a while to master and can't be learned, or implemented, in five minutes, but they help me focus on the major areas that produce the best results.

"The point of being a Five-Minute Fundraiser is that I can quickly make the call on whether the Ingredients of *Asking Rights* are in place for a new initiative or a new investor.

"Fundraising Skills turn an immense endeavor—you've probably heard that some capital campaigns take years—into more manageable tasks. Because we use *Asking Rights* concept, our campaigns are measured in months, not years.

"Another reason Fundraising Skills are so important is because they are the pivotal link that transforms a potential funder into an actual investor.

"They offer tangible evidence people can observe for themselves while learning about an organization's mission and strategic vision for the transformational use of their money. If they like what they see in how we run our campaign, people typically assume we run our business in the same efficient and effective manner, which makes the idea of investing much easier to rally around."

"I think I understand," said Marley. "During a campaign, you are the face of the organization."

"Exactly," agreed John. "But it's more than that. The Five-Minute Fundraiser has to not only organize and manage the campaign, which we'll talk about in a minute, she also needs to be able to succinctly explain our Outcomes so they make sense to a potential investor or the investment in the organization won't be made...or won't be made at the significant level expected."

"Lastly," said Janet, "a person's skills in this area can make or break a campaign. Even the highest Credibility and the best Outcomes cannot overcome an unorganized campaign, unprofessional interactions, or being unprepared for an *ask*.

"That's why the Five-Minute Fundraiser concept is so important to an organization. I need to not only connect with investors, I need to manage the process."

"Which is why I get so nervous when she starts talking about retiring," John said.

Janet smiled as she asked rhetorically, "So what are the most important Fundraising Skills?"

She wrote Overall Campaign Management under the Ingredient headline.

"This skill is not only the ability to see the big picture, but also to structure the effort in the right way. There are so many people involved, most of whom have busy personal and professional lives beyond their association with our organization, that it really does become the proverbial 'herding cats' scenario.

"I think in our last campaign—five years ago—we had 18 volunteer leaders involved, a fact that offers a perfect segue to the next necessary skill."

Marley was scribbling notes and noticed John glance at his watch. She looked up and saw Janet noticed it too.

"Let me just get through the Fundraising Skills Ingredient," Janet said, "and we'll break for lunch."

"I'm not trying to rush you...too much," smiled John.

"I know," replied Janet, and then turned to look at Marley. "One of the skills needed by a Five-Minute Fundraiser is Interpersonal Skills," she said, turning to write the same phrase on the sheet in front of her.

John nodded in obvious appreciation. "Janet's perceptiveness is just another credit toward her success as our Five-Minute Fundraiser," he said.

"She's aware that we've been in this room awhile, it's close to lunchtime, and we've covered a lot of ground."

"Is 'perceptiveness' one of the official Fundraising Skills?" asked Marley.

"Not specifically, but let's come back to that," Janet said, smiling as she wrote Leadership Cultivation and Enlistment on the sheet.

"This skill is important to a campaign for obvious and not so obvious reasons.

An obvious reason is that the 'right' leaders need to be cultivated because they are the names and faces of the effort.

"They will carry the message to the community and their influence opens doors to critical funding sources. Sometimes, they are natural choices because of their commitment to the mission. But even then, these leaders need special attention during a campaign, which is why Cultivation is the perfect term to describe the process. Often we start with only a seed of interest and must nurture it into active campaign engagement."

John added, "Enlistment as a campaign leader, actually signing people up to participate in the effort, is the prize of proper Cultivation. Here's where things might be not so obvious.

"A person's position in a campaign must be commensurate with his or her investment, which can be a bit tricky. Some want to be very visible, but they don't want to make the appropriate, leading investment. If what they bring to the campaign has other value—like access to other community leaders and/or potential investors—exceptions might be made. But, as a rule of thumb, the higher the position of leadership in the campaign, the larger the investment."

Janet added, "It's important that campaign leaders understand they 'lead' the way for others not just by participating in the effort, but that others will calibrate their level of investment to those at the top of the campaign. It's just human nature."

John agreed, "I want to underscore what Janet just said. Let's say we evaluate a potential investor at $100,000 and cultivate her for a campaign leadership position commensurate with that amount. Then, let's say, she offers to invest only $10,000, substantially below and only 10 percent of where we evaluated her. We may not offer her that particular leadership position as it will set a bad precedent for the rest of the campaign. If everyone else did the same thing, we would only be at 10 percent of our overall campaign goal, no matter what the goal might be. That's not what we would consider a successful effort."

"What do you mean 'evaluate'?" asked Marley.

"That's our next point," answered Janet. "Prospect Evaluation is another skill that has a direct effect on the amount of dollars we raise. In the early stages of a campaign, we evaluate prospective investors in terms of a realistic investment they might make. But we don't do it in a vacuum; we use the knowledge of others in the community to help us.

"We use these investment assessments, combined with the information gleaned through the feasibility study, to determine an achievable goal for the campaign."

Janet turned back to the sheets on the wall and wrote Leveraging Investors under Fundraising Skills.

"By Leveraging Investors," she said, "I mean we move from the top down in a campaign...from the largest investor to the smallest. If we start out with the right investments at the top and at the very beginning of a campaign, those asked to subsequently participate will reference the people and investments above them to help determine their own commitment. Not only do we leverage investments this way, we also do it by industry sector, size of company or foundation, and relative wealth."

"I didn't realize fundraising was so…scientific," Marley puzzled aloud.

Janet and John nodded in unison at her assessment.

John said, "Wait until we talk about the third Ingredient—Outcomes—and how investors value them. But Leveraging Investors is what makes an effort a true campaign rather than just a series of isolated, individual *ask*s. A campaign allows a planned process to unfold and, as it does, momentum to build toward the goal. It also reinforces collegiality and teamwork."

"Speaking of momentum," Janet chimed in. "Remember how I noticed a few minutes ago that it was probably time for a break when John glanced at his watch?"

Marley nodded.

"I didn't know if he was bored or hungry or just needed a break, but I knew I had lost his attention for a minute. Being able to read nonverbal cues is an important element in any job but especially in fundraising," Janet said as she tapped her marker on the words Interpersonal Skills under the Fundraising Skills headline.

"And to be a Five-Minute Fundraiser," she continued, "there are definitely certain professional traits required."

"Like what?" asked Marley.

"You were a finance major, right?"

Marley nodded in answer to Janet's question.

"Well, a Five-Minute Fundraiser is like an investor relations person in the corporate world, a person who keeps investors informed of what's going on in the organization. It's important to be attentive to investors, communicate often, and make them feel like their investment is appreciated and impactful.

"I know every one of our investors, and old school fundraising would have you believe this professional rapport is why people give the organization money. But for significant sums of money—not the one-off bake sales or the 3 Gs—it really does take more than just knowing someone. People give because they want to see something they care about—their community, their fellow citizens— succeed. Communication skills, sincerity, and empathy are important traits in many professions, but they are especially critical in fundraising."

John jumped in. "I've seen a lot of people fail at fundraising because of their lack of Interpersonal Skills. They aren't good at time management—for example, being late for a meeting at which you plan to ask for money is, typically, lethal—or they talk more than listen, which can also be lethal during the investor cultivation process. It's simple stuff really, but you'd be surprised how many fall short."

Janet nodded her support of this point. "Speaking of the *ask*, if there is a moment in the entire campaign process that encompasses being a successful Five-Minute Fundraiser, that's it.

"If you think about it, the *ask* is the culmination of all the hard work that occurs in the other areas of Fundraising Skills, and it rests on the other two Ingredients—Credibility and Outcomes. If everything else is done correctly, quite a number of people can get to the *ask*—and be successful—but there is also the potential to fail at the finish line."

"Why is that?" asked Marley.

"John and I have spent many hours pondering the same thing," answered Janet, "and we don't know how to describe it other than it centers around fear."

"Fear of what?" Marley responded.

"Fear of being told 'no,'" said John. "That's why many people do not do well in sales. They're afraid of being told 'no.'"

"In organizations like ours," said Janet, "we are so close—so connected to our mission and what we do—that being told 'no' often feels like potential investors are rejecting us personally."

"Of course, they're not," said John, "but it's easy to feel that way.

"The other part is that, so often, fundraisers can feel that there is no way a potential investor could say 'no,' but then they—seemingly unexpectedly—do."

"We work so hard on building our Credibility," Janet said supportively. "We have great Outcomes, spend a lot of time on Cultivation and Enlistment, connect them to what we do, evaluate them at the appropriate level, and so on. Yet, they can decide not to invest in our organization.

"Being told 'no' after what can be months or even years of effort is, naturally, difficult to digest."

"I get it," said Marley. "I guess being able to deal with rejection comes with the territory. And I can see how the potential for that reaction can be kind of scary if your campaign—if your job—depends on securing investments."

"Yes, but you can't let the chance of 'no' scare you out of making the *ask*," said Janet.

"Let's go back to the guiding principles of the Five-Minute Fundraiser and certain concepts that make the job of raising money easier.

"If we focus on Credibility, Fundraising Skills, and Outcomes, the chance of being told 'no' is really minimized. In fact, I can't remember the last time I heard a flat out 'no.'

"Most of the time, if I do hear it, it's because the potential investor doesn't feel connected to our Outcomes. In these cases, a person may prefer to invest in other organizations, which is why the Ingredient we will start with after lunch—Outcomes—is so important."

"Before we break, though," John prompted, "we need to get to the Critical Fundraising Advantage for Fundraising Skills."

"Good point, John," Janet agreed. She stepped up to a blank sheet and wrote as she spoke: "The Critical Fundraising Advantage of Fundraising Skills is it closes the deal."

"That," smiled Marley, "is self-explanatory."

John and Janet smiled with her. "With that," he said, "let's meet back here at 2:00 p.m."

"Perfect! What a great morning," Janet said as she looked at the sheets and thought about all they had discussed.

And Marley, feeling she might have found her calling, nodded enthusiastically in agreement.

Fundraising Skills Takeaways

Fundraising Skills are important because they:
- Allow the other Ingredients—Credibility and Outcomes—to be monetized
- Turn an immense endeavor—like a capital campaign—into more manageable tasks measured in months instead of years
- Are the pivotal link that transforms a potential funder into an actual investor
- Can make or break a campaign

What are the most important Fundraising Skills?
- Overall Campaign Management
- Interpersonal Skills
- Leadership Cultivation and Enlistment
- Prospect Evaluation
- Leveraging Investors

What is the Critical Fundraising Advantage of Fundraising Skills?

It closes the deal.

The Three Ingredients

The Third Ingredient: Outcomes

"**O**utcomes are the third and final Ingredient of *Asking Rights*," started Janet, as soon as all three were back in the room after lunch.

She walked over to the remaining two sheets hanging on the wall and wrote Impact on Our Customers' Lives under Outcomes.

"Of all of the Ingredients, I feel Outcomes are the most important because they represent the impact we have on people's lives. But there is another reason they are important.

"They are the real reason, ultimately, people give money to nonprofits."

As Janet was writing The Reason People Give Money to Nonprofits on the sheet, John chimed in.

"This concept cannot be emphasized enough," he said. "Old-school fundraisers have said for years that the reason people give to nonprofits is because of connections between individuals.

"On top of that, those same 'experts' say that giving is an emotional act. While connection is certainly important and emotions can be powerful, at the end of the day, Janet and I believe people give money to nonprofits because they want to see good things happen, things they care about.

"And since I've never met a person yet that likes to see their money wasted, the reason they are ultimately giving money is because of an organization's Outcomes."

"It really is a different way of thinking," added Janet. "It forces me to look at my job as more than simply a master networker. When you approach fundraising as just relationship building, you spend all of your time doing that, and I feel it really minimizes the other things we do…namely delivering valuable Outcomes."

The next phrase Janet wrote on the current sheet was Tangible Proof that We are Making a Difference.

"The critical thing about Outcomes is they can be measured," she said. "They can be analyzed and objectively demonstrated, so it's not just us—the nonprofit—saying we do great things. An independent third party can validate them."

Moving to the blank sheet, she labeled it How We Utilize Outcomes.

"What I mean by this,' said Janet, "is that I use them all the time in a fundraising context. It's a big part of my job."

Marley leaned forward. "I'm beginning to understand why Outcomes are so important and how they contradict 'old school' thinking—as you've said—that connections are more important."

"Exactly," replied Janet. "That's why so many organizations struggle with their fundraising. They tend to focus on 'the way it's always been done,' spending a lot of time on the 3 Gs we talked about earlier as well as some form of an annual campaign, which is how they keep their doors open."

"We don't even do an annual campaign," interjected John. "We used to, but we found that if we run a more organized, Outcomes-based, multi-year pledge campaign, we raise far more money in less time. We don't rely on emotional appeals, tax deductions, or aggrandizements. We base our *ask*s on Outcomes and it works beautifully."

"What other nonprofits have failed to fully grasp," continued Janet, "is that their donors—again, we call them *investors*—have become much more educated and sophisticated in recent years. They use third-party evaluators like Charity Navigator and GuideStar. They look up our Form 990 from the IRS and study our website."

"There are so many nonprofits to give money to," Marley offered, "and so many ways to give money today...by mail, in person, online, by text, calling in response to a TV appeal..."

"Yes, yes, all those and more," agreed Janet. "What it all adds up to is that what people are truly lacking is not information on our budget or on our activities or on our customer case studies—it's information on our Outcomes!"

The first words Janet wrote under How We Utilize Outcomes were Focus on Outcomes, Not Outputs.

"They're not basically the same thing?" asked Marley.

"Many nonprofits seem to think they are, but they are very different," John answered. "And the more we differentiate between the two, the more—and more significant—investments we receive."

"Outputs are measures of activity," explained Janet. "Outcomes are the impact we have on our customers.

"For example, the number of meals served, the number of classes taught, or the number of animals rescued are Outputs. They tell potential investors how busy an organization is. What they don't tell is the difference an organization is having on its customers' lives."

"What would be examples of Outcomes in those same cases?" asked Marley.

"Great question," said Janet. "It's not how many meals, but how those meals enabled people to get healthy again so they could continue to work or stay in school. It's not how many classes were taught, but how those classes allowed people to get their diploma so they could get a good paying job. It's not how many animals were rescued, but the far-reaching consequences avoided by spaying or neutering those animals, getting them the necessary shots to keep them free from disease, and how those things help the root problems that will eventually lead to fewer animals needing to be rescued in the future."

Outputs
tell an investor
how busy an
organization is.

Outcomes
tell an investor
the difference an
organization makes.

"I can see why that approach really resonates with people," said Marley.

"We also Tie Outcomes Directly to Funding," Janet said as she wrote the same phrase on the sheet.

"We tell our current and potential investors how much money it will take to achieve a desired Outcome. This takes a funding goal out of the fuzzy area of 'we just do the best we can.'"

"We also work hard at communicating our Outcomes to investors," said John. "We don't take for granted that they know, and we also use language they understand and appreciate. They are not 'in the trenches' like we are, so we can't assume they know all our jargon."

"Remember when you first walked into my office?" Janet asked. "I was working on a new Investor Relations piece for our annual meeting.

"If an organization is going to truly embrace the concepts of *Asking Rights*, it has to do more than 'talk the talk.' It has to 'walk the walk.' That's why we take keeping our investors informed about how their investments in our programs and services are performing very seriously."

The next concept Janet wrote on the sheet were Make Sure Outcomes are Valued by Investors.

"I'd like to think that we are pretty smart people around here," she said, "but we can't assume we know what our investors value. And if we don't know if they value the Outcomes we deliver, we can't expect them to fund them."

"So how do you know?" asked Marley.

"Simple," said John. "We ask them."

"Exactly," Janet agreed. "Before a campaign, we conduct what's called a feasibility study to share our intended Outcomes and get feedback on them.

"I know we mentioned the study earlier, but never really explained it. The study is when we schedule one-on-one meetings with current and potential investors because their feedback—about the Outcomes and the organization—is completely confidential, which ensures as much honesty as possible.

"If the Outcomes we propose are valued by those we interview, then we move forward with asking for investments in them during the campaign. If they aren't valued, then we get feedback on how to make them valuable."

John added, "Since campaigns only happen every four to five years, we don't wait for one to ask if our Outcomes are valued. I meet with all of our significant investors personally at least once a year. The Investor Relations piece we mentioned earlier also serves as a way to keep our investors and our community informed on progress toward the stated Outcomes."

Janet wrote her last phrase on the sheet: Make Sure Outcomes are Investable.

"This topic is a longer discussion than we have time for today," she said, "but I can hit the high points pretty quickly.

"By *investable* I mean we make sure each Outcome we discuss with investors meets the basic criteria of being worthy of their money. One criterion they need to pass is the 'reasonableness' test. We can't promise too much, and we have to be realistic about how much it will cost to deliver or fulfill an Outcome.

"Another criterion is that the Outcome can be described quantitatively in one way or another. This ensures we can measure our progress.

"And the most important criterion, in my opinion, is that the dots from funding to Outcome can be easily connected."

"I agree with the importance of that one," said John. "If I'm asking potential investors for $500,000 of their hard-earned money, I have to be able to explain to them quickly how their investment will lead directly to the delivery of an Outcome they value.

"Investors have to be able to easily see the path to success, and the shorter, more direct that path is, the easier it is to get significant investments."

This time it was Janet who glanced at her watch. "I can't believe this day has gone by so quickly," she said. "But the time has come to tie a bow around Outcomes.

"Its Critical Fundraising Advantage is…it justifies the amount of the *ask*."

Marley furrowed her brow. "Do you mean Outcomes determine how much money you ask someone for?"

"Yes," said John, "but, as with many things in fundraising, it's a little more nuanced than that."

Janet picked up on that point. "If we make sure to focus on Outcomes, not Outputs—communicate them, relate them directly to the funding need, ensure they are valued by investors, and ensure they are investable—then, yes, Outcomes have a big influence on the amount of money we ultimately ask for from investors.

"Of course," she continued, "we need to follow the Cultivation, Enlistment and Evaluation principles we shared with you earlier today before we get to the point of asking anything from a potential investor.

"But if everything lines up as it should, the better the Outcomes—and the more they are valued by investors—the more right we have to ask them for money.

That's why we call the concept *Asking Rights*."

"And we have to earn those rights every day," John stated emphatically.

"So," John looked at Marley, "how do you feel about what we've shared with you today?"

Marley smiled and said, "It's a lot to digest, but it makes perfect sense to me. It's no wonder you're so successful at not only fulfilling your mission, but also in securing the money to make it happen.

"I really appreciate the time you both have taken to explain it all to me."

"Our pleasure," said John. "But we did it for a reason. Given your extensive research into nonprofits and the interest you've shown us yesterday and today, Janet and I think you might be a good candidate to join the organization and work with us to learn how to be a Five-Minute Fundraiser.

"Janet's a great mentor, and we need to be able to transfer all of her institutional knowledge before she really does decide to retire," John said wryly.

Janet smiled and said to Marley, "Think about all we covered today, let it sink in how differently we approach fundraising and, more broadly, how we achieve financial sustainability.

"Give John a call at the beginning of next week if you would like to discuss the possibility of joining our team. If so, we can set up a time to meet with you again."

"Thank you!" said Marley. "I really do appreciate your time and attention.

"Before I leave, would you mind if I take pictures of the sheets? I'd like to have a reminder of all of this great information you were kind enough to share with me."

"Be our guest," replied Janet. "We'll hang on to them too. Presenting these concepts and principles really does have a way of distilling a lot of information into concise bullet points.

"Marley, we thank you for your time and attention as well."

Outcomes Takeaways

Outcomes are important because they:
- Demonstrate Impact on Customers' Lives
- Are the Reason People Give Money to Nonprofits
- Are Tangible Proof that a Nonprofit is Making a Difference

How We Utilize Outcomes
- Focus on Outcomes, Not Outputs
- Tie Outcomes Directly to Funding
- Make Sure Outcomes are Valued by Investors
- Make Sure Outcomes are Investable

What is the Critical Fundraising Advantage Outcomes provide?

It justifies the amount of the ask.

The Five-Minute Fundraiser Ties It All Together (Why Ingredients Matter)

For the next few days, Marley thought long and hard about her visit with John and Janet. She really liked what she heard during her time with them, and the opportunity to learn from someone like Janet seemed like a rare opportunity.

The Monday following their daylong meeting, Marley called John.

"I would like to take you up on your offer to learn more about the way your organization raises money and how my skills might be able to support funding your mission," she said.

"Wonderful," said John. "I want to make our next discussion a little less formal in that I don't want to talk so much about the Ingredients and aspects of *Asking Rights*.

"Instead, I want to talk about how we apply them in our fundraising strategy, both tactically and strategically.

"To do that, I'll share some of our 'in the trenches' fundraising stories. From there we should be able to make a more informed decision as to whether we want to move forward with you as part of the team.

"How about this Wednesday at 1:00 p.m.?"

When Marley arrived that day, she was genuinely excited to learn more and nervously optimistic about her chances to work for the organization.

When she entered John's office, she noticed something she hadn't before. His office wasn't filled with industry awards or pictures with clients and local dignitaries or souvenir gala trinkets like she had seen in the offices of other executive directors.

What she did see was the sheets from their previous discussion now hanging on his walls.

John greeted her warmly. "Did all of the information we heaped on you last week make sense? I apologize if it was a little too much detail. After you left, I looked at all these sheets and realized we covered a lot of ground."

Marley replied, "To be honest, I did have to go over some of those pictures I took several times, but each time I did it made more and more sense."

"Well," said John, "I hung them up in here today to remind us of all we discussed and, more important, to help guide our conversation today about how we put these Ingredients into action.

"Why don't we start with you telling me your three major takeaways from last week."

Marley had anticipated this question. "I learned that a nonprofit—although it may have the legal right to ask people for money—may not have earned *Asking Rights* to seek the money necessary to become financially sustainable. That was probably my biggest takeaway."

"Tell me more," said John.

"I learned the three Ingredients of *Asking Rights* are Credibility, Fundraising Skills, and Outcomes, and that each has multiple key components as well as a Critical Fundraising Advantage.

"I also learned that Five-Minute Fundraiser, while not a literal term, is a concept and a process that allows great fundraisers to focus on the most important things, such as communicating with investors on a regular basis and ensuring the organization's Outcomes are truly valued by current and potential investors, especially in today's fast-paced, social media-obsessed society."

"Wow," cheered John. "You certainly got the correct takeaways. Did we even mention social media last week or the reduced attention span of today's investors, who are constantly bombarded with nonprofits asking for money by saying they do 'wonderful' things?"

"Not specifically," said Marley, "but that's my version of what I heard applied to the next generation of donors, err…investors.

"I was thinking, with more and more dependence on technology, it's probably inevitable that more and more fundraising will be done that way.

"And, in light of that, I can see how Credibility, Fundraising Skills, and Outcomes will be even more important in the future than they are now. They are the Ingredients that will create the winning recipe for success and differentiate one nonprofit from another."

John was impressed. "That's a very inspired way of looking at fundraising. I like the way you see the future of it through the lens of *Asking Rights*."

"Thank you!" beamed Marley. "I'm really excited to hear some of your 'in the trenches' stories so I can better understand how the Ingredients work in practice."

"Well then," said John. "Let's get started."

Putting Credibility to Work

"**A**s we shared last week, it all begins with Credibility," he said.

"The term can be interpreted broadly, but when applied to the Five-Minute Fundraiser, the focus sharpens."

"Can you share an example of Credibility in a fundraising context?" asked Marley.

"Absolutely," John replied. "There once was a young fundraiser who was conducting a feasibility study for a youth organization in the state of Tennessee. On a particular appointment, he was set to interview a bank president and was ushered into a large, well-appointed office. During the interview, the fundraiser thought he was doing a great job and was expecting a strong indication for a future commitment from the prospect.

"When the fundraiser finally got to the question about possibly investing in the program, the banker surprised him with this answer: 'Why would I give you, or the organization you represent, any money? I don't know you or the organization. I don't know what you do or who you help. I don't know where you are located or who sits on your board. You haven't earned the right to ask me for money!'"

"Oh, what an unpleasant surprise," Marley frowned.

"Exactly!" agreed John. "Having been on hundreds of feasibility interviews, I know the feeling of thinking it's going well, only to have the rug pulled out from under you at the end. But better to have this happen during the study than in the campaign, when you are counting on an investment."

"I can see how that could really hurt a campaign," Marley acknowledged.

"If it happens with the highest potential investors," explained John, "it can destroy a campaign because it could scare off the rest of the potential investors. But I'm getting ahead of myself.

"You may have guessed that experience actually happened to me, and that costly lesson became the genesis for the concept of *Asking Rights*, which, in a nutshell, is *earning* the right to ask for money."

"Is that why Credibility is one of the three Ingredients?" asked Marley.

"It sure is," John replied. "Remember, the Critical Fundraising Advantage of Credibility is that it gets you in the door.

"Where that really comes into play, especially for a newer or smaller nonprofit that wants to launch a campaign, is during the feasibility study when key interviews with community leaders are sought."

"Can you explain more about a feasibility study?" asked Marley.

"Of course!" John said. "I sometimes get carried away on this topic and forget that not everyone knows our industry's jargon.

"That question—about a basic element of the capital campaign process—is a good reminder to ensure, especially when speaking with current and potential investors, we use language that helps people quickly understand the ultimate goal."

John drew a deep breath. "Before any nonprofit jumps into a fundraising campaign, they need to do a feasibility study. People may use different names for it, like 'goal assessment' or 'opportunity analysis,' but it's the same process.

"The term 'feasibility study' also means something completely different to an engineer, a marketer, or an environmental scientist. In the fundraising world, it is the process of meeting with potential investors, presenting a plan of work, gathering feedback, and analyzing all that feedback to determine a course of direction.

"The feedback—pros, cons, and everything in between—is what becomes the blueprint for a successful campaign."

"I understand," Marley said. "And I would guess, if I'm interviewed for a feasibility study, I would want to know the end result and how my feedback influenced the plan?"

"Exactly!" boomed John. "Keep that in mind as we talk more about those initial feasibility study interviews, and Credibility's Critical Fundraising Advantage of getting in the door.

"You see, nonprofits are usually really good at heading in the direction dictated by their missions. Finding the money to support their missions, well, they're typically not so good at.

"They also tend to feel that a capital campaign is the answer to all their financial problems, because all of the galas and golf tournaments they host are not getting them there.

"When they get turned down for those critical feasibility study interviews— again and again—they get very frustrated. That frustration turns into disappointment when they realize that if they can't even get an interview with someone, they will probably not be able to count on them as a future investor.

"So, getting those initial interviews with potential investors, where an organization can present its plans and needs and the expected Outcomes, is the acid test of Credibility."

A well-done
feasibility study
becomes the blueprint
for a
successful campaign.

"Ah…so Credibility literally *and* figuratively gets you in the door with potential investors," said Marley.

"Exactly, but as we shared last week," John continued, "it also helps with attracting and retaining board members and staff. It helps with recruiting volunteers, with referrals for our programs and services, and it helps by making campaigns shorter in duration, since people know about and have confidence in our organization, which makes the decision to invest with us easier."

"With it having such an effect on internal and external situations, I completely see why Credibility is so foundational," said Marley.

"Exactly," said John. "For the Five-Minute Fundraiser, Credibility is a means to an end.

"And, to put it bluntly, the end is people actually pulling the trigger and writing a check. When they know who we are, what we do, who sits on our board, who we help, and how well we help them, the job of raising money is made so much easier."

Marley nodded in understanding. "As you shared, nobody likes to see their time, talent, or treasure wasted on inefficient organizations or questionable efforts."

"No, they don't," said John. "And they certainly won't write a check to an organization that doesn't inspire confidence."

Putting Fundraising Skills to Work

"I'm assuming, then, that you have more war stories about Fundraising Skills than any of the other Ingredients?" suggested Marley.

"We certainly have many of them," John responded. "Some are humorous, some are not, but all of them are instructive.

"Let's start with the Cultivation of campaign leaders. I know we've talked about—and it would seem obvious that—the 'right' leaders must be in place for a capital campaign to succeed, but how they are recruited is more complicated."

"Complicated how?" Marley asked.

"I'll give you a real example from personal experience," answered John.

"In a campaign for the nonprofit I worked for before this organization, I served in the same position as Janet does now…Director of Development.

"The feasibility study was conducted by an outside consulting firm, which ensured the confidentiality of the interviews and objectivity of the feedback analysis.

"The consultant told us we needed a certain person to be chairman of the campaign. This person was head of a local utility company, which was in the process of being taken over by a larger utility company, and I agreed he was the right person.

"This leader was well-respected, had the cachet of being a large employer in our community, his likely investment was at the top of the list, and he certainly had influence with others in the community.

"To be honest, it didn't take much effort to convince him that he should be our chairman. He wanted the job. The problem was, because his company was in the midst of being acquired, he couldn't commit himself or his company financially.

"As a finance major, you likely learned there are laws about materially changing a company's balance sheet prior to being purchased. So, even though he wanted to help, he simply couldn't.

"We were faced with the decision to either wait out the acquisition and risk losing momentum for the campaign, or move on with our second choice to be chairman."

"What a dilemma!" Marley agreed. "What did you do?"

"Well, to make things even more complicated," answered John, "our next choice was wavering on whether she could give the time commitment necessary for the campaign. She was the head of a local law firm and, although she supported us, she had a very active practice and her time was in short supply. She could say 'yes' or 'no,' we just weren't sure."

"What would have been the harm in asking her anyway?" Marley asked.

"Good question," said John. "In a small town, word gets around quickly. If a potential leader for a campaign turns us down, and then another does, by the time we get to the third or fourth person, people start to feel unimportant because they are farther from the first to be asked.

"I know it may sound silly, but human nature is human nature. And when we are talking about the level of investment being proportionate to a person's leadership position in the campaign, it can start a downward trend that is difficult to reverse because there are only so many viable options in a small community."

"I'm on pins and needles for how it turned out!" said Marley.

"It actually could not have turned out better," John replied. "We waited until the utility companies merged so our first choice was free to become chairman, and we went over goal on the campaign!"

"Whew," Marley exhaled. "I was hoping for a success story."

"Another interesting situation," said John, "but one that we can often maximize, is Prospect Evaluation. Once a capital campaign is underway, one of the first things we do is meet with people in the community who know the giving preferences and patterns of other community leaders and well-to-do citizens. We have them look over prospect lists to help us determine potential campaign roles and investment amounts.

"There is actually a rating system where prospects are graded by their previous giving history, their capacity to give, their connection to the organization, and so on.

"Banks are a great example of how we can often turn what might seem to be an unfavorable situation into one that helps our fundraising."

"Are banks always on the prospect list?" asked Marley.

"Almost always," John replied. "You don't really have a community without a bank, even in the age of the Internet. It's been that way since the old west, when a town only really had to have three things: a bank, a saloon, and a jail."

"And the first two often led to being a patron of the third," Marley joked.

"Very likely true," John laughed.

"So, what is the unfavorable situation related to banks that you mentioned?" asked Marley.

"Banks are very sensitive to their relative size," said John. "They always know how much their competitors have in deposits, loans, and so forth. When it doesn't look like one of the larger banks will be much of a supporter, it's an opportunity for a smaller bank to make a big splash, especially if they just had a change in management, which banks often do."

"I'm not sure what you mean by a big splash?" she asked.

"By 'big splash' I mean the opportunity to be a leader in a campaign, making an investment potentially much larger than the size of their business might suggest. In other words, a new manager at a smaller bank can make quite a name for herself or himself by being a campaign chairperson, understanding that this position of high visibility carries with it the expectation of a large, if not the largest, investment. It is certainly a way to introduce oneself to the community in a very big, very positive way."

"I see what you're saying," Marley said.

"Asking for a potential financial commitment," continued John, "is another one of those Fundraising Skills about which I could go on and on.

"But, in brief and in general, we refer to it as the *ask*. There is a lot of work that comes before an actual *ask* can be made. The Evaluation process we mentioned, Cultivation, and so on.

"But what I want to focus on are two important things relating specifically to the *ask*: Motivation and Excuses."

Marley was really interested in this topic. "I was hoping we would talk about Motivation, since I didn't remember discussing it last week."

John nodded. "We didn't get to it yet, which is why I want to spend some time on it today. It's one of the areas I, personally, find intriguing because when we are asking people to part with their hard-earned money, Motivation becomes very important."

Marley offered, "With all that you and Janet have shared, I completely understand this now. And I know you are not big fans of the 3 Gs, so I wondered how Motivation plays into your fundraising appeals."

"At the most basic level," said John, "it's been said that people give money to a nonprofit for either altruistic or selfish reasons. I think there is a better way to say it.

"I think people are motivated to give from an either emotional or rational place...or somewhere in between. It has to do with the way our brain is hardwired through evolution—our personality, our personal experience in this world—and even the kind of day we might be having."

"Does it also matter how much money is being talked about?" Marley asked.

"Very astute," beamed John. "It certainly does."

"So which Motivation do you cater to at this organization?" she asked.

He replied, "We do whatever works for the individual or the situation, but we definitely skew toward the rational side, especially since we are usually asking for larger sums of money compared to other nonprofits.

"As an example," John continued, "think back a few years. You were sitting in the comfort of your own home, watching a prime-time show, and it breaks to a commercial where the first image you see is an abused dog, chained outside in the cold."

"I remember that commercial!" Marley exclaimed. "And there was a really melodramatic song sung by a very popular female artist playing in the background."

"Exactly!" John agreed. "Would you consider that a successful appeal for your money?"

"Well, on one hand, I remember it after all of these years. On the other hand, I didn't leap off of the couch and write them a check, so...I guess not?" she answered tentatively.

"Let me change the question," John replied. "Would you consider it an emotional appeal for your money or a rational one?"

The motivation to give
is not always
exclusively
emotional or rational.

It is often a mix of both.

"Emotional. 100 percent. No doubt about it," Marley replied.

"So, you remember it, which is good from an advertising perspective, but it didn't incite you to action," John continued. "In fundraising, would you call that a success or failure?

Marley started to respond, but John stopped her.

"Wait! Don't answer that yet. Let me change the question.

"You throw a fabulous gala for your organization every year. People rave about it, talk for days about how much fun they had, and it always sells out all of the tables in the venue.

"Unfortunately, it only raises about four percent of the organization's budget and takes an inordinate amount of staff time—months and months of planning— to pull together. Would you call that a fundraising success?"

"I guess I couldn't," Marley replied. "Seems like a lot of effort for very little return…to me."

"I agree," John said. "That doesn't necessarily mean that events based primarily on emotional appeals don't work. They have worked for years, but they are becoming less and less effective. And in my experience, the larger the *ask*, the less effective an emotional appeal becomes."

"Why is that?" Marley asked.

"I could talk for hours on that topic," he answered, "but let me summarize by saying that emotional appeals are a race to the bottom.

"Let's take that commercial we mentioned earlier. What are they going to do next time…show a dog being euthanized? I don't mean to be graphic, but I think that investors are so much more sophisticated these days, and they want something much more substantial, like Outcomes, to inspire their meaningful investments."

"I see your point," she nodded.

"I will say, in defense of emotional appeals," John continued, "that decision-making comes from the same part of the brain that controls emotions: the limbic system. That's why sometimes people say things like 'it doesn't feel right' when making a decision to do something or not.

"But when we ask people to make a decision to invest in an organization, what helps them to say 'this feels right' and make a much larger investment is the rational information we provide, like how valuable the Outcomes are to them and their community. It gets them to think about the nonprofit's value in ways they might not on their own."

"So, you start with an emotional appeal and close with a rational appeal?" Marley asked.

"Not necessarily," John replied, "but, in general, that's how it often happens. We just tend to move on to the rational messaging sooner because we have found that the faster we do, the more money we raise."

John paused to look at the sheets from their meeting.

"Let's move on to Excuses. When you're asking people for their money, they will be very creative—and convincing—with their reasons for saying 'no.' Janet and I have heard every reason under the sun. That's where a mastery of Fundraising Skills is critical."

"You mean people don't just tell you 'no'?" Marley looked confused.

John smiled. "They naturally don't want to do that, especially when we talk about investing in the important work we do here. It's just human nature."

"I guess I thought they would be more up front for that very reason," said Marley. "After all, you're doing important, valuable things for this community, a community of which they are members, so I wouldn't think they would want to lead you on."

When people are asked
to make a decision
to invest in
an organization,
what helps them decide
is rational information
…how valuable
the Outcomes are
to them and
to the community.

John grinned knowingly.

"They don't really lead us on, they just get very creative with their reasons to say 'no,' or send strong signals that they will say 'no' in the future, when a campaign is in full swing.

"During a feasibility study, people know why we are coming to speak with them. They know that one day in the future we may ask them to help fund the project or initiative. They also know we are not looking for a firm commitment during the interview, just an indication of a potential investment level.

"So, the interview is their first opportunity to manage our expectations about becoming an investor in our organization. Since they know ahead of time that we will be discussing a potential future investment, they have the opportunity to be creative in their reasons not to invest.

"For example, one of the most common reasons is 'we already committed the money in our philanthropic budget for the next few years.'

"Another is 'I'm just about to go on the board of another nonprofit, so I need to direct my money to them.'

"Business people will often say things like 'business is down right now' or 'cash flow is tight' or even 'we need to keep these types of commitments off our balance sheet.'

"These can certainly be valid reasons, but more often than not, they are simply excuses. And a Five-Minute Fundraiser can typically tell whether these excuses are genuine. So, we have learned to make the *ask* in several different ways—like making it conditional on performance or, at the very least, setting up another time to discuss the potential for investment after we've had time to formulate good responses to their concerns."

Marley asked, "Does it sometimes mean the Credibility Ingredient is not as good as you might have thought, at least in their eyes?"

John nodded thoughtfully. "It very well could mean that, but since we're already in the door, which is the Critical Fundraising Advantage of Credibility, more often than not it tells us they really don't understand the positive impact of our Outcomes and their downstream ripple effects.

"It tells us that we need to get them more connected to our organization and more aware of our impact in the community. That's precisely why we spend so much time developing and communicating our Outcomes, which is the next area we will discuss."

Putting Outcomes to Work

"**O**utcomes. Outcomes. Outcomes," chanted John. "Those are the three rules of fundraising.

"Just like 'location, location, location' are the three most important elements of retail. Or at least they used to be before the Internet made bricks and mortar locations somewhat obsolete."

"You have said all along that Outcomes are the most important Ingredient," Marley chimed in.

John nodded in appreciation. "Exactly. So, let's go back to the abused pet commercial, the emotional appeal we discussed.

"The commercial's implication is the organization works to eliminate the suffering those pets experience. And it ran nationwide, which is something the typical nonprofit can't afford.

"If you subscribe to our theory that rational appeals raise more money, then the commercial would have been more effective if it said how many pets the organization actually saved from suffering, maybe a comparison of how much better it was at this result than the local dog catcher, how efficient it is with money, how it educates the community to help break the cycle of abuse, and so on."

"Doesn't that detract from their message?" Marley asked. "The commercial *is* pretty powerful between the images and the music."

"Ah, therein lies the rub," John acknowledged. "It's a big debate in the fundraising industry. Which works better: the emotional or the rational appeal? The organization's Credibility lets it get away with just a purely emotional appeal, but— as you said—the commercial didn't inspire you to act. So, the appeal left money on the table.

"Your reaction to adding rational elements—that it would detract from the message—is very perceptive, and academics from some very good schools have studied this topic for years."

The 3 Rules
of Fundraising:

Outcomes!
Outcomes!
Outcomes!

"Really? What did they find?" Marley asked.

"First," John offered, "let me say I disagree with their findings, not because of the results themselves, but because the assumptions made along the way that directed them to a conclusion are very much divorced from reality.

"To determine whether emotional or rational appeals worked better in a fundraising situation, they approached individuals on a college campus sitting alone in the student union.

"After the individuals agreed to participate in the exercise, each person was given five $1 bills and told they would be given two scenarios describing severe hunger conditions. After hearing the descriptions, they were asked to 'vote' for the more effective appeal with their dollars."

"In other words, they could donate to one of the two options or split up the money any way they wanted?" Marley asked.

"Yes," John nodded. "The first scenario was a picture of a girl who was obviously suffering from hunger. It was paired with a narrative that named her and described the conditions she faced.

"The second scenario was a page of statistics describing how many people lived in the region and—just like the girl in the first scenario—the conditions they faced.

"Which scenario do you think got the most in donations?"

"Well," Marley hedged, "this might go against your theory about emotional appeals not being effective, but I would give the girl in the first scenario the money. I mean, she would have been staring right at me from the picture! So, I guess she got the most donations?"

"You are exactly right," John conceded. "And so is your reasoning. They called her the 'humanized victim,' and it's easy to understand why that scenario spoke to more people than the page of statistics did.

"The conclusion of the academics was that the *emotional* appeal was, therefore, more effective than the quantitative appeal, or what we call the *rational* appeal."

"So that proves the contradiction of your theory then, doesn't it?" Marley offered tentatively.

"On the face of it, yes, but not really," John shook his head.

"The disconnects from reality are numerous," he explained. "First, the amount of money was immaterial and second, it wasn't even their money, so they had no real skin in the game.

"More important, they were not connected to the organization that was going to deliver the hunger relief or the cause they were asked to donate to, and without those connections—in the real world—significant, impactful money does not get raised.

"But the disconnects alone aren't why I believe emotional appeals are not as effective as rational appeals. The scenario representing the rational appeal used uninspiring numbers on a page. Statistics about hunger are not the same as Outcomes delivered. There's a big difference."

"I want to make sure I understand this right," Marley said. "You're saying that just offering an emotional appeal potentially leaves money on the table and offering facts like statistics doesn't automatically make a rational appeal effective?"

"Exactly," John agreed. "Think back to the commercial about abused pets. Would you give money when shown pictures of abused dogs or when you were shown a sheet of paper listing how many dogs were suffering the same fate, the number of injuries that were reported, etc.? Would the numbers on a page have moved you to act and send them a check?"

"Of course not," she said. "The pictures of the pets would get my dollars, just like the picture of the girl suffering from severe hunger would."

John shrugged. "OK, but what if the alternative to the pictures was how many animals the organization helps, how far it can stretch dollars, the unique way it mobilizes rescue efforts, the care it gives animals while in protective custody, and—ultimately—how many animals it saves from being euthanized by putting them into loving homes?"

"*That* would get my money," Marley offered enthusiastically.

"Those...are Outcomes!" proclaimed John.

"I totally get it," she nodded vigorously.

"So, you see how effective they are?" he said. "Outcomes dynamically connect you to the organization and that connection is much stronger than a picture or static stats.

"But I'm not done yet," John continued. "I need to tell you how we make our Outcomes irresistible.

"To do that," he smiled, "we make them investable."

As if on cue, Janet walked into the room.

"Perfect timing," said John. "We were just getting ready to jump into Investable Outcomes™.

"We've been through the idea of emotional versus rational appeals and how the approaches have a deeper effect on fundraising than it may seem at first glance."

"Great," said Janet. "Investable Outcomes are the most effective way I know to raise money—in greater amounts and in shorter time periods. If you want, I can take the discussion from here?"

"Be my guest," John said.

"I'll pick a somewhat complex example to illustrate my point," started Janet.

"Certain areas like health and education are relatively easier to raise money for than, say, building a performing arts and cultural center, so I'll go with that."

Janet sat across from Marley. "Let's say we have never had such an arts center in our town, and we are tired of being in the shadow of the big city that is 20 miles away.

"We want to attract the kinds of shows and events that right now we have to travel to the city to see—fighting traffic, hunting for a place to park, etc.—and we want to reap the economic benefits of having such events locally.

"We have the moral support of the businesses, the city council, and the community in general. Our estimate is that we'll need $30 million to build the center of our dreams."

"Does 'your' organization have *Asking Rights*?" prompted John.

"In fact, we do not," said Janet, shaking her head. "So, we know it is vitally important that we make the project's Outcomes investable.

"Our main Outcomes are that we want to bring world-class events to town so we are recognized as an area that supports the arts and we want our school system to be recognized as one that understands the importance of the arts in education. To that end, we plan to utilize the center as a satellite classroom.

"We also want businesses to be able to attract an educated workforce, which the diversity of entertainment provided by the arts will help them to do."

Marley interjected. "I understand your Outcomes, but how do you make them investable?"

"Great question," Janet smiled. "First, we need to make sure they pass the 'reasonableness' test.

"In other words, are they reasonable to most people given our mission, budget, etc. This qualifier is probably the weakest of all for the organization since we don't have a facility like this now, and we have never raised anything close to $30 million before.

"It's difficult to say if most people will think this is a 'reasonable' endeavor, but our predictions of attendance are conservative and our ability to attract quality events is realistic, so we have done what we can to be as realistic as possible.

We will need to do a feasibility test to find out more.

"Next up is whether our Outcomes provide an acceptable 'return on investment' or ROI. We have done some preliminary work to determine this and, if we conservatively evaluate what the community will likely reap in terms of notoriety, educational enhancements, workforce attraction, and improvements to quality of life, we feel the value will exceed the cost of the facility in less than five years."

"That's a very good payback period," John offered.

"Agreed," said Janet. "Now the dots being easily connected from funding to Outcomes is another indicator of them being investable.

"Do we feel we've done a good job of explaining how an investor's money will be directly responsible for creating a facility that will lead to world-class events, better arts education for our children, and quality hires for our local businesses?

"I think we have ensured each of the three major Outcomes has its own rationale and backed them up with solid quantitative examples.

"Last, if investors value Outcomes, they will be more likely to write a check to fund them. It's a very plain and straight forward proposition."

"How do we ensure that they are valued?" asked Marley.

"Not by assuming we know," answered Janet. "And not by taking for granted they think like the staff or the board does.

"We know this by talking to them and asking them. This is a key element of the feasibility study. The results of that study will serve as the blueprint for making our Outcomes appealing and motivating— even coveted—by investors."

Investable Outcomes:

Pass the
'reasonableness' test

Provide a 'return
on investment'

Allow investors
to 'connect the dots'
between funding
and Outcomes

Are 'valued'
by investors

"Excellent example, Janet," John approved. "And very impressive, given you made it up on the spot."

"Thanks, John," she smiled. "When you come into work every day thinking about how to make Outcomes investable, which you do when you're a Five-Minute Fundraiser, it becomes second nature."

John nodded in agreement. "Let's end this part of the discussion about putting Outcomes to work by explaining why they're so important."

He looked at Marley. "As we shared before, the Critical Fundraising Advantage for Outcomes is it justifies the amount of the *ask*.

"So, the better the Outcomes—the more they are investable, the more they are valued by investors—the more money we raise.

"With all that in mind, it's still true that Outcomes have to be understandable and relatable to the prospect.

"Let me give you the last example we'll cover for today."

John nodded toward Janet. "To continue with Janet's example of the performing arts center, putting the Outcomes in terms that make sense to an employer in the engineering industry, for example, is critical to getting that employer behind the effort.

"Simply telling them that we will host world-class events may not resonate. They may not personally be a patron of the arts or have children in the school system.

"What will get them interested is the way in which we craft the message— backing it up with facts—on how it might help their business. That is the avenue that will get them connected to the campaign, which is critical."

"How do you do that?" Marley asked.

"We ask about how many of their employees have expressed an interest in the arts," said John.

"We talk about how facilities such as this have been shown to be important to the types of employees they are seeking. We talk about the value of reducing their hiring time, which we show them in black and white, based on the information we gleaned from the feasibility interview with them."

"This is so interesting," marveled Marley. "I had no idea that this approach even existed. All the other nonprofits I researched seemed to focus on the 3 Gs!"

Janet nodded in understanding. "There's a lot to learn, but if you keep the tenets of the Five-Minute Fundraiser top of mind, it becomes so much easier," said Janet.

John looked at Janet, who nodded her approval, and then turned toward Marley.

"So, Marley, does our way of doing business sound interesting enough for you to consider coming on board with us?" asked John.

"It certainly does!" she nodded enthusiastically.

"Great!" said John. "I'll get back to you with our offer next week."

"This is wonderful," Marley exclaimed. "Thank you so much!"

Becoming a
Five-Minute Fundraiser

The next few days passed quickly for Marley. She couldn't help but wonder about the offer John would extend.

Would she make a good Five-Minute Fundraiser? It was such an innovative way of thinking!

Could she keep up with a mentor like Janet? She felt she could.

When the phone finally rang, she made an effort to ensure her nervous anticipation wasn't obvious.

"Hello John," she said.

"Hello Marley! I have some great news for you," he said. "Janet and I have talked it over and we would like to offer you the opportunity to work directly with her, learning to be a Five-Minute Fundraiser. If all goes well, you would be right in line to take the reins when she retires. How does that sound to you?"

"It sounds just like what I've been looking for!" exclaimed Marley, knowing this organization is where she could make a difference in the world and change lives.

And so, Marley began her journey to becoming a Five-Minute Fundraiser.

Your Next Steps

The concepts offered in "The Five-Minute Fundraiser" are an introduction to the more detailed information presented in Tom Ralser's *Asking Rights* book series. These concepts are part of the many ways in which he helps nonprofits, their boards, and—most important— their fundraising efforts succeed and thrive.

The next step for most organizations is a customized workshop led by Tom for senior staff and board members. If you want to learn more on your own, consider using the workbook "Developing Your Asking Rights," available on Amazon, as a guide.

If you would like additional information about how we can help your organization, please reach out to:

Tom Ralser
tralser@ConvergentNonprofit.com
800-886-0280
Convergent Nonprofit Solutions
ConvergentNonprofit.com

About the Author

Tom Ralser pioneered the concept of applying for-profit principles to nonprofit fundraising. Through this methodology, he has helped organizations raise more than $1.8 billion over the past two decades by focusing on the Outcomes they deliver, which is ultimately why most people invest in nonprofits.

His Investment-Driven Model™ of fundraising led him to develop the Organizational Value Proposition®, a litmus test widely used by corporations, foundations, and individuals to ensure the organizations in which they invest are truly delivering Outcomes with value, as well as the concept of Investable Outcomes™, which has helped nonprofits around the world raise more money in less time.

Having worked with hundreds of nonprofits in all 50 states, Tom is frequently asked to be the keynote speaker at for-profit and nonprofit industry conferences. He is a founding partner of Convergent Nonprofit Solutions, a Chartered Financial Analyst, and author of the best-selling books: *ROI for Nonprofits: The New Key to Sustainability*, *Asking Rights: Why Some Nonprofits Get Funded (and some don't)*, and its companion workbook *Developing Your Asking Rights*.

Afterward

Excerpt from
Developing Your Asking Rights, published in 2016

According to the National Center for Charitable Statistics, approximately 1.56 million nonprofits were registered with the Internal Revenue Service in 2015, an increase of 10.4 percent from 2005.

That means the competition for 'time, talent and treasure' is fierce. More than that, volunteers and investors are becoming increasingly savvy—and choosy! —about where they spend their resources.

Asking Rights is not an abstract concept. It's a proven strategy that—when embraced and employed by the various stakeholders of a nonprofit—can bring about remarkable change.

Organizations that embrace this methodology become financially sustainable; find new sources of revenue; are able to fund new initiatives; become more accountable and transparent; can more easily test new initiatives for support; are able to recruit new leadership; deliver more meaningful Outcomes; and become true community assets.

The concepts in all of these books are critical and timely for any nonprofit that wants to not just survive, but thrive. They are designed to keep the perspective of the nonprofit investor in mind, which is critical for long-term success. Adopting the perspective of the nonprofit investor does not guarantee success, but it increases the likelihood your nonprofit will fully fund its mission and continue to have the ability to deliver valuable Outcomes.

Made in the USA
Columbia, SC
25 February 2023

12972422R00074